Good Lord, Deliver Us

A Lenten Journey

40 Days of Lent

Leonard W. Freeman
Lindsay Hardin Freeman

Forward Movement
Morehouse Publishing

FORWARD MOVEMENT, an official, non-profit agency of the Episcopal church, is sustained through sales and tax-free contributions from our readers.

Cover design: Albonetti Design

Library of Congress Cataloging-in-Publication Data

Freeman, Leonard W.
  Good Lord, deliver us : a lenten journey : 40 days of Lent / Leonard W. Freeman, Lindsay Hardin Freeman.
     p. cm.
  ISBN 978-0-88028-325-0 (soft cover)
  1. Lent—Meditations. 2. Easter—Meditations. I. Freeman, Lindsay Hardin. II. Title.
  BV85.F66 2010
  242'.34—dc22

                        2010045418

Printed in the United States of America

Morehouse Publishing
NEW YORK · HARRISBURG · DENVER

FORWARD MOVEMENT
412 Sycamore Street, Cincinnati, Ohio 45202-4195
800-543-1813   www.forwardmovement.org

Introduction

The path for our Lenten journey this year will be guided largely by the thirty-two petitions of the Great Litany, the first English language rite prepared by Thomas Cranmer, Archbishop of Canterbury in the sixteenth century. The Great Litany is traditionally read or sung in Episcopal congregations on the first Sunday of Lent.

In Cranmer's translation and revisions the Great Litany reflects a searing penitence and dependence upon God amidst dangers both physical and spiritual. Despite differences in time and place, Cranmer's deep sense of human frailty and holy grace speaks to the underlying cares, concerns, and aspirations of our human hearts, and to the sources of wisdom, guidance, and strength for our steps along this pilgrim path.

To complete our Lenten journey, beginning with Monday in Lent 5 we will reflect on the wisdom of the Great Vigil of Easter and Holy Week lessons that reach back into the oldest roots of our scriptural tradition. The Bible readings and Collects of the Great Vigil, typically read in darkness, recall God's saving acts, beginning with Creation. Together with the traditional readings for Holy Week, they illuminate for us the rocky path to Calvary and the glorious rising of Easter Day.

As a married couple we have written these reflections to flow back and forth between our voices.

—Leonard W. & Lindsay Hardin Freeman

The Great Litany

(*The Book of Common Prayer,* pp. 148-152)

O God the Father, Creator of heaven and earth,
Have mercy upon us.

O God the Son, Redeemer of the world,
Have mercy upon us.

O God the Holy Ghost, Sanctifier of the faithful,
Have mercy upon us.

O holy, blessed, and glorious Trinity, one God,
Have mercy upon us.

Remember not, Lord Christ, our offenses, nor the offenses of our forefathers; neither reward us according to our sins. Spare us, good Lord, spare thy people, whom thou hast redeemed with thy most precious blood, and by thy mercy preserve us for ever.
Spare us, good Lord.

From all evil and wickedness; from sin; from the crafts and assaults of the devil; and from everlasting damnation,
Good Lord, deliver us.

From all blindness of heart; from pride, vainglory, and hypocrisy; from envy, hatred, and malice; and from all want of charity,

Good Lord, deliver us.

From all inordinate and sinful affections; and from all the deceits of the world, the flesh, and the devil,

Good Lord, deliver us.

From all false doctrine, heresy, and schism; from hardness of heart, and contempt of thy Word and commandment,

Good Lord, deliver us.

From lightning and tempest; from earthquake, fire, and flood; from plague, pestilence, and famine,

Good Lord, deliver us.

From all oppression, conspiracy, and rebellion; from violence, battle, and murder; and from dying suddenly and unprepared,

Good Lord, deliver us.

By the mystery of thy holy Incarnation; by thy holy Nativity and submission to the Law; by thy Baptism, Fasting, and Temptation,

Good Lord, deliver us.

By thine Agony and Bloody Sweat; by thy Cross and Passion; by thy precious Death and Burial; by thy glorious Resurrection and Ascension; and by the Coming of the Holy Ghost,

Good Lord, deliver us.

In all time of our tribulation; in all time of our prosperity; in the hour of death, and in the day of judgment,

Good Lord, deliver us.

We sinners do beseech thee to hear us, O Lord God; and that it may please thee to rule and govern thy holy Church Universal in the right way,

We beesech thee to hear us, good Lord.

That it may please thee to illumine all bishops, priests, and deacons, with true knowledge and understanding of thy Word; and that both by their preaching and living, they may set it forth, and show it accordingly,

We beseech thee to hear us, good Lord.

That it may please thee to bless and keep all thy people,

We beseech thee to hear us, good Lord.

That it may please thee to send forth laborers into thy harvest, and to draw all mankind into thy kingdom,

We beseech thee to hear us, good Lord.

That it may please thee to give to all people increase of grace to hear and receive thy Word, and to bring forth the fruits of the Spirit,

We beseech thee to hear us, good Lord.

That it may please thee to bring into the way of truth all such as have erred, and are deceived,

We beseech thee to hear us, good Lord.

That it may please thee to give us a heart to love and fear thee, and diligently to live after thy commandments,

We beseech thee to hear us, good Lord.

That it may please thee so to rule the hearts of thy servants, the President of the United States (*or of this nation*), and all others in authority, that they may do justice, and love mercy, and walk in the ways of truth,

We beseech thee to hear us, good Lord.

That it may please thee to make wars to cease in all the world; to give to all nations unity, peace, and concord; and to bestow freedom upon all peoples,

We beseech thee to hear us, good Lord.

That it may please thee to show thy pity upon all prisoners and captives, the homeless and the hungry, and all who are desolate and oppressed,

We beseech thee to hear us, good Lord.

That it may please thee to give and preserve to our use the bountiful fruits of the earth, so that in due time all may enjoy them,

We beseech thee to hear us, good Lord.

That it may please thee to inspire us, in our several callings, to do the work which thou givest us to do with singleness of heart as thy servants, and for the common good,

We beseech thee to hear us, good Lord.

That it may please thee to preserve all who are in danger by reason of their labor or their travel,

We beseech thee to hear us, good Lord.

That it may please thee to preserve, and provide for, all women in childbirth, young children and orphans, the widowed, and all whose homes are broken or torn by strife,

We beseech thee to hear us, good Lord.

That it may please thee to visit the lonely; to strengthen all who suffer in mind, body, and spirit; and to comfort with thy presence those who are failing and infirm,

We beseech thee to hear us, good Lord.

That it may please thee to support, help, and comfort all who are in danger, necessity, and tribulation,

We beseech thee to hear us, good Lord.

That it may please thee to have mercy upon all mankind,

We beseech thee to hear us, good Lord.

That it may please thee to give us true repentance; to forgive us all our sins, negligences, and ignorances; and to endue us with the grace of thy Holy Spirit to amend our lives according to thy holy Word,

We beseech thee to hear us, good Lord.

That it may please thee to forgive our enemies, persecutors, and slanderers, and to turn their hearts,

We beseech thee to hear us, good Lord.

That it may please thee to strengthen such as do stand; to comfort and help the weak-hearted; to raise up those who fall; and finally to beat down Satan under our feet,

We beseech thee to hear us, good Lord.

That it may please thee to grant to all the faithful departed eternal life and peace,

We beseech thee to hear us, good Lord.

That it may please thee to grant that, in the fellowship of [_____ and] all the saints, we may attain to thy heavenly kingdom,

We beseech thee to hear us, good Lord.

Ash Wednesday

"Watchful active waiting…"

As a middle-aged man sitting down to begin these Lenten reflections, I find myself recently diagnosed with an illness for which one of the options is "watchful active waiting." On Ash Wednesday morning, at the start of the Lenten journey, it strikes me that this may be a particularly appropriate pathway. The ashes of this day remind us of several things, one of which is our own mortality. Ashes to ashes. Dust to dust.

We are all in a period of watchful active waiting. The question is: waiting for what? In the Middle Ages some monastic communities dug an open grave on the grounds between their chapel and the refectory so that the young monks would always be aware of their common earthly destination on the way to their heavenly home. "Live each day, each moment, as if it were your last, so that you fill it with things of value," it could be said. All material things end in a grave, so place your hope and value in things of the soul.

It can sound a bit macabre. What strikes me most as I stand at the front edge of Lent is that what we are watchfully waiting for are not signs of our own mortal end, but signs of the resurrection. For that, of course, is where Lent goes. Good Friday is not the final piece of the journey. Easter is.

What signs of the resurrection do you see around you? What signs of new, larger, fuller life do you see breaking in, as a promise and first taste of what can and will be, for our world and ourselves? —*LWF*

Thursday after Ash Wednesday

Remember not, Lord Christ, our offenses, nor the offenses of our forefathers; neither reward us according to our sins. Spare us, good Lord, spare thy people, whom thou hast redeemed with thy most precious blood, and by thy mercy preserve us for ever.

Spare us, good Lord.

Thomas Cranmer, whose pen crafted the Great Litany, knew the meaning of these phrases on a level deeper than most.

Cranmer was a brilliant editor, scholar, theologian, and priest. But he was also a man caught in the crossfires of his time, as Reformation ideals clashed with the precepts of the Roman Catholic Church.

Cranmer believed in the king's sovereignty in all matters, both civil and religious. That belief led to his appointment by King Henry VIII as Archbishop of Canterbury, where he was instrumental in reforming the worship and doctrine of the Church in England. The architect of *The Book of Common Prayer*, Cranmer worked diligently to integrate reformed understandings into the life and worship of the English people.

Cranmer was tried for treason and imprisoned during the reign of Roman Catholic Queen Mary (aka Bloody Mary). Under pressure, he recanted many of his reformed beliefs. Led to the pulpit of St. Mary's Church in Oxford on March 21, 1556, Cranmer stood before the congregation, poised to recant publicly. But he would not sink to that task. Instead, he renounced his earlier recantations and proclaimed his love for Christ.

Yanked from the pulpit and tied to the stake, he thrust his right hand into the flames, saying, "This hand hath offended!"—for with it, he had penned the denials of his beliefs. Out of the ashes was born a saint.

Lord, by the end of our lives, may we too have contributed mightily to the building up of your kingdom.
—LHF

Friday after Ash Wednesday

From all evil and wickedness; from sin; from the crafts and assaults of the devil; and from everlasting damnation,

Good Lord, deliver us.

Legend has it that while jailed, Thomas Cranmer was marched up to the roof of his Oxford prison and forced to watch the executions of his good friends and colleagues Hugh Latimer and Nicholas Ridley.

Like him, they had been caught in the trials of the times. Like him, they had preached the faith as they understood it. Like him, they struggled to be faithful.

It wasn't that they were lightweights, always fluttering in the direction of the latest doctrinal winds. Latimer was a gifted preacher, one of the most popular of his day. Ridley was chaplain to Archbishop Cranmer and then bishop of London.

Refusing to turn their backs on their faith, Ridley and Latimer were brought to the stake to be burned in October of 1555, after months of imprisonment in the Tower of London. There, Latimer uttered his famous words: "Be of good comfort, Master Ridley, and play the man; we shall this day light such a candle by God's grace in England as shall never be put out."

During this Lenten season, let us be especially mindful of the courage displayed by our forebears and find ways to share our faith with others. —*LHF*

Saturday after Ash Wednesday

From all blindness of heart; from pride, vainglory, and hypocrisy; from envy, hatred, and malice; and from all want of charity,

Good Lord, deliver us.

For many of us, Lent means embracing certain disciplines. Some may say that tradition is outdated, that it is better to "take on" something. Perhaps.

However we choose to observe Lent, the key is to do something. Jesus went into the wilderness for forty days, preparing himself for the rigors of ministry. Solid footing for him involved solitude, fasting, and rejecting temptation.

Moses prayed and fasted before he climbed Mount Sinai to receive the Ten Commandments. Sarah faced thirty-five years of wilderness trials before she gave birth to Isaac, the joy of her life and the future of Israel. Hildegard of Bingen, the twelfth-century mystic, fasted so that she could see more clearly visions of the Divine.

Sacrifice is more than a thread through biblical history. It is a solid pillar. Through discipline we gain inner strength so that we are stronger in trying times and better equipped to follow the One who truly leads.

For those who take on something extra in Lent: if it works, go for it. But for others of us, additional duties threaten to chip away at our souls. Sometimes purpose and clarity fade away like a fizzling firecracker when the "to-do" list becomes too long.

And *that* is where the temptations—things like pride and hypocrisy and vainglory (great word!) are most likely to strike—when we run the race while trying to keep too many plates spinning.

God, grant that we might learn to do more with less, stripped away all that is nonessential for life in your Son. —*LHF*

First Sunday in Lent

From all inordinate and sinful affections; and from all the deceits of the world, the flesh, and the devil,

Good Lord, deliver us.

The world, the flesh, and the devil—the classic and unholy trinity over against the gifts of Father, Son, and Holy Spirit—is a parallelism wherein each dark deceit comes as a twist of the true.

The Trinity is the deep expression of how we experience the one Lord in our lives. God the Father, Creator, is God experienced through the natural world, the truth of science and nature, the truth of the miracle I know in the birth of my child, the innate resonance of my heart to a sunset scene.

God the Son is God known through human story and history. We are a people of stories; it is where we go to *re*create in film or book, to touch life's inner meaning, finally encapsulated in the archetypal story of Jesus.

And the Holy Spirit is the experience of God within us—as we trust in that deep voice pushing, prodding, leading, and guiding us.

From these the unholy trinity would twist our hearts away. The world—as if nature and rocks were *all* there were—turns sourly into "survival of the fittest" and "nature red in tooth and claw." The flesh transforms our human story into a pornographic novel, with sensation the only reality. And the devil, the destroyer, is that other who would suck at our souls to turn us toward despair and heartsickness.

Whereas there are "ordinate" and appropriate affections in our lives that God loves and provides for us, the deceits just draw us down and away from our true selves and true hope.

Good Lord, deliver us. —*LWF*

Monday in Lent 1

From all false doctrine, heresy, and schism; from hardness of heart, and contempt of thy Word and commandment,

Good Lord, deliver us.

It was the 1980s and the heyday of the Peace Movement. I was riding in a taxicab with former Iranian hostage Moorhead Kennedy on the way to a church speaking engagement. "You know," he said, "there are places in the church I could get up in the pulpit and deny the resurrection and nobody would blink…but if I questioned the Nuclear Arms Freeze they'd hang me. The problem," he went on, "is that the hawks and the doves are really the same people… they never produce real peace, because they're so convinced that they have the total corner on truth that they demonize the other side."

Contempt and hardness of heart can take us down some dark paths. In the church I have seen a lot of "issues-du-jour" trump reason, community, compassion, and theology, to everyone's loss. If we hold other viewpoints in contempt—leaving no room for grace or the possibility that we might not have everything right ourselves—then peace and cooperation and real movement forward come to a screeching halt. When we care so much about an issue that we see nothing of value in the opposing view and those who espouse it, we veer toward schism.

A seminary professor explained heresy to me as "a piece of the truth that gets taken for the whole thing." And that is its problem. The part that is true seduces us into seeing it as the *only* reality, dismissing other viewpoints and other people.

Hardness of heart as often comes from good motives as bad.

Lord, help me to care enough to act, but also not to fall into contempt so that I get in your way. —LWF

Tuesday in Lent 1

From lightning and tempest; from earthquake, fire, and flood; from plague, pestilence, and famine,

Good Lord, deliver us.

As I write, one of the poorest nations on earth is suffering from the effects of a disastrous earthquake. Almost every building on the island has been knocked down or askew. The airport is so ruined that relief planes cannot even land to bring aid. It is horrendous. We send off checks, call in prayers, anything we can think of to help.

So many prayers have gone up that the local TV news is doing a Good Question segment on "Does communal prayer make a difference?" Good question indeed.

And, of course, in a year's time, or six months or a decade, another such disaster will hit. Nature's harms seem endless. And they raise the question "Why?" to nature's Master, Creator, Redeemer.

Even nature needs redemption. We can forget that. In our ecologically friendly age we can sometimes forget that we may not be on the same agenda as mother nature. Our survival depends on hers, and I suspect she needs us at least not to blow the earth out of orbit and into oblivion. But if I understand it rightly, the earthquake may be for mother nature a necessary stretching of the arms, as it were; a release of tectonic plate pressure for the planet's good. Isn't a lot of what we see as disaster just nature's correcting of some other imbalance?

Our cry of help to nature's Creator is not only a recognition that we are dealing with things beyond our human control, but also a plea for the Creator of both nature and ourselves to stand with us and for us, come what may. —*LWF*

Wednesday in Lent 1

*From all oppression, conspiracy, and rebellion;
from violence, battle, and murder; and from dying
suddenly and unprepared,*

Good Lord, deliver us.

We were talking about dying. It was not theoretical. Sheila had been going downhill with cancer for a year now, and the end was near. We had gathered with family and talked in private. She would not be dying "suddenly and unprepared."

And yet, resting on a couch, the glassed-in porch an oasis of nature and warmth, she suddenly verbalized an anxiety: "Len, I don't know how to die."

A silence. What do you say? "Me neither"? And then something came. "I don't think we have to know how to die. Dying just happens to us. Our job is to live—every moment we have."

All deaths are in some way unprepared. And none of us can really know the moment or time. The list for today—unlike the pestilence and plague of yesterday's petition—is of man-made horrors. Violence, battle, and murder result from our human decisions. We can strive to create a world where they are less the norm, where oppression and rebellion do not rule the day, where at least the manner of dying has more dignity to it, and less horror.

But the actual dying will happen to us all. And our job is to do the living. To the last breath.

Am I prepared? In the sense of living each moment as strongly and faithfully as I can? As an agent of the living God? As a soul with hope? —*LWF*

Thursday in Lent 1

By the mystery of thy holy Incarnation; by thy holy Nativity and submission to the Law; by thy Baptism, Fasting, and Temptation,

Good Lord, deliver us.

It is one thing to ask for help. It is another to know from where—by what means—help comes. These next two days articulate why, and from where, we Christians see help coming.

Today's petition outlines the hope raised in us from Jesus' story up to the Passion. It is that sense of Jesus' life—expressed for some in the acronym WWJD (What Would Jesus Do?)—as the guide for our daily lives and actions. This is partly Jesus as ethical teacher and guide, the learned sage in whose life even nonbelievers can find wisdom and guidance.

But for us it is more.

Jesus, coming into human form, provides us an actual picture of what the best of human life can be.

This is the Son of Man, after all, the archetypal image of what God intended humans to be from the beginning. Do we want to get it right? If we pattern ourselves on this picture—given from heaven—of what and how we are meant to live, then even the worst that life can dish out will not defeat us. Because he is not just another good man but a promise from the Creator.

Cranmer's petition resonates with the power of Saint Patrick's "Breastplate," the great hymn of protection:

> *I bind this day to me for ever,*
> *by power of faith, Christ's Incarnation;*
> *his baptism in the Jordan river;*
> *his death on cross for my salvation*

—*THE HYMNAL 1982, #370*

We can ask Jesus for help because of who Jesus is. Not naively, but out of deepest trust. "We are *bold* to say: Our Father…" because of what the mysteries of the Incarnation and Jesus' own example tell us is possible. —*LWF*

Friday in Lent 1

By thine Agony and Bloody Sweat; by thy Cross and Passion; by thy precious Death and Burial; by thy glorious Resurrection and Ascension; and by the Coming of the Holy Ghost,

Good Lord, deliver us.

Several years ago, Mel Gibson's film *The Passion of the Christ* set a number of people's teeth on edge. The images were so graphic, so brutal—agony and bloody sweat, torture and horror—that many eyes turned away, turned off. Part of the problem was that for many of us "gentle Jesus meek and mild" had become a much more comfortable image. A person dying so horribly on our behalf raises problems for us when we want to consider Jesus *only* from the standpoint of his ethical teachings. Then we aren't sure what to do with the cross and resurrection parts of the story.

But there they are, and they lay down an exclamation point that is indeed a stumbling block and a scandal, for if this part of the story doesn't make some sense, then what we have is one of the best, most evolved, intelligent, moral human beings ever on the planet simply being done in. And where is the promise and hope in that?

Our faith is that, somewhere in what C.S. Lewis called the "deep magic" of life, this sacrifice has changed things for the rest of us.

I am not always sure about the "how" of it. Theologians posit several theories. My understanding is not required, but rather my accepting and appreciating.

The horrors I can read about every day. The gifts of forgiveness and resurrection and the Spirit are what pull me through them. —*LWF*

Saturday in Lent 1

In all time of our tribulation; in all time of our prosperity; in the hour of death, and in the day of judgment,

Good Lord, deliver us.

In times of our "prosperity." That's a stopper. I didn't expect that in the list of things from which I need deliverance.

Then again, we've just come through a period of what we thought would be unendingly prosperous times in our country, and it's turned a bit ashes-ey in our mouths. Profligate, rather than profitable, turns out to have been the apt word for the early years of the twenty-first century. And of course we all played.

The problem with prosperity is that we start to believe our own press notices: that we are masters of our own fates, deserving of all our blessings, and that our comfort is really just our due and the appropriate measure of human progress.

That prosperity as well as disaster can pull our hearts away from God is a well-told tale in the Bible. Remember "it is easier for a camel to go through the eye of a needle than for someone who is rich to enter the kingdom of God" (Matthew 19:24). It's probably not an accident that pornography and drugs and crime statistics have risen along with the Gross National Product.

God does not want us to be impoverished—starvation and degradation do nothing for the human soul—but that you and I remember the real priorities of our lives in the midst of prosperity. When things are going well is precisely the time that I'm not too good at prioritizing.

Lenten self-denial may be pointed right at this. Step out of our prosperity and comfort modes even a little bit, and things can get clearer. —*LWF*

Second Sunday in Lent

We sinners do beseech thee to hear us, O Lord God; and that it may please thee to rule and govern thy holy Church Universal in the right way,

We beseech thee to hear us, good Lord.

I grew up with an alcoholic father. Try as he might, he was never able in this life to solve his addiction. I trust that God has worked with him since death and that he has found healing. Redemption has come to the rest of the family as well, through much work and even more grace.

As a result of growing up in that environment, I've had to work on my humility. When you're in an alcoholic family, there are many barriers. You're often on your own, especially if you're a child. Adults often seem to be masquerading as grown-ups. Sometimes children are the responsible ones, trying to keep their heads low and not draw attention to themselves, trying to stay under any radar, avoiding conflict and spontaneous rage.

Such an upside-down understanding of things follows children of alcoholics into their adult lives. They continue to say to themselves: "I've got to be right. It's the only way I know. I'm the only one I can trust."

One of the great lessons of life and maturity is that I don't always have to have it right. Sometimes I can be wrong.

It's a big admission, accepting our vulnerability. But that kind of humility and openness is what God wants in both our relationships with each other and in our relationship with him. Once we have a sense of our own fallibility, it's much easier to invite God to "rule and govern thy holy Church Universal in the right way." It's also a relief. Someone Else is in charge.

—*LHF*

Monday in Lent 2

That it may please thee to illumine all bishops, priests, and deacons, with true knowledge and understanding of thy Word; and that both by their preaching and living, they may set it forth, and show it accordingly,

We beseech thee to hear us, good Lord.

We consecrated our new bishop here yesterday. The Minneapolis Convention Center was alive. Clergy and laity seemed happy, uniformly and unusually happy. Four years of developing a diocesan-wide vision of ministry was complete. Barriers had been broken down, relationships developed. Some

150 clergy, vested in albs and red stoles, stretched out behind various committees, drummers, dancers, and banner-carriers.

Then a silver-haired man, wearing a leather jacket, walked up and nudged one of us at the end of the line.

"Is this the gay and lesbian convention?"

"What?" we said, jarred.

"You heard me. Is this the gay and lesbian convention?"

"No."

"That's all you Episcopalians talk about."

That's all we talk about?

Really. The hopes of a diocese stretched in front of us. The joy of a people gathered spilled out. The sage being burnt by Native Americans as an initial blessing, a cleansing, wafted through the air.

We talk about a lot more. Most of all, we talk about Jesus.

The cynics are there. Those who would destroy us walk among us, needling, poking, tearing down. Yet our call as God's people is to build up, to illuminate, to set forth "thy Word," to celebrate it among us, to share our joy. To talk about Jesus.

The man walked away. We moved forward, shaking the dust from our feet, reminding ourselves to rejoice, to know the Center of our being. —*LHF*

Tuesday in Lent 2

That it may please thee to bless and keep all thy people,
We beseech thee to hear us, good Lord.

It was supposed to have been a really good day. But it wasn't, especially for the unfortunate circus performer.

I'd taken my sons, ages eight and twelve, to the Excel Center in St. Paul to see the circus. I love circuses: the big animals, the acrobats, the clowns, the smells.

We sat there, mesmerized. One act after another came on, and then three women dancers, dressed in flowing white outfits, ran and jumped on ropes that stretched from the ceiling. Acrobatic and muscular, they ascended while doing somersaults and vaults in unison. My eye was on the middle rope. It was close to where we were sitting.

Then the unthinkable happened. Out of the corner of my eye I saw the woman on the left fall, trailed by her rope, about forty feet to the hard concrete floor.

Circus people ran out. The announcer noted there had been an injury and asked for prayers. Then, as emergency workers worked over her, the clowns were sent in to entertain the crowd, to distract the children.

Later that night, her death was announced on the news. I have not been to a circus since.

In the middle of life, death. In the middle of joy, tragedy.

God, we don't always understand pain and suffering and death. We know there are no guarantees, but we continue to pray that you would bless and keep us—in this life and in the life to come, where you promise that all tears are wiped from our faces. —LHF

Wednesday in Lent 2

That it may please thee to send forth laborers into thy harvest, and to draw all mankind into thy kingdom,

We beseech thee to hear us, good Lord.

One of my jobs during college was to work "on the line" for the Green Giant Company in southern Minnesota, processing thousands of ears of corn in twelve-hour shifts during the fall harvest. Sitting under a loud husking machine that shot out corn cobs incessantly, I would arrange them to point the same way on the conveyer belt.

When the floor boss wanted to get my attention, she bounced a corn cob off my helmet. Despite her attitude and the endless tedium, this job, and others like it, got me through college.

I am one of the lucky ones. Others have worse jobs. Some have no job at all.

One of the most remarkable agrarian workers in biblical history is Ruth. Newly widowed, she joins her cranky and demeaning mother-in-law, Naomi, on a forty-mile wilderness trek back to Naomi's hometown. Starving and homeless once they reach Bethlehem, Ruth finds unpaid work in a farmer's field, harvesting bits of grain left behind. Day after day she returns, keeping her head low.

One thing leads to another. Through a series of coincidences and Naomi's meddling, Ruth marries the owner of the field, Boaz, and has a son: the father of King David. And many years later, in the same town, Jesus is born. Through Ruth and others, Jesus has non-Jewish blood, drawing all humankind into God's kingdom.

Often we cannot see ahead to the results of our efforts. But if we do an honest day's work, whether at home or afield, and stay open to the Spirit, we can help lay down the bedrock for generations, making an eternal difference. —*LHF*

Thursday in Lent 2

That it may please thee to give to all people increase of grace to hear and receive thy Word, and to bring forth the fruits of the Spirit,

We beseech thee to hear us, good Lord.

It is easy to jump over the first part of this phrase and careen merrily toward the fruits of the Spirit: love, joy, peace, patience, kindness, generosity, faithfulness, gentleness, and self-control (Galatians 5:22-23). At first glance, those words seem light and fluffy.

But marshmallows they are not. They are built on the foundation of two actions: an increase of grace and a receiving of the Word.

First, grace. Tertullian, the early African church father, defined grace as divine energy working in the soul. Through the centuries, theologians have refined that definition, but it is a wonderful place to start. Cranmer, through his grasp of sacramental theology, added that God offers grace freely through the sacraments and such grace acts in the recipient over time.

Second, the Word. Not "word," but "Word" with a capital W. As in the Word became flesh: Jesus. That people may receive God's Word. That people may receive Jesus.

Divine energy. Receiving Jesus. The point is that we are changed by God, through grace. Receiving divine energy, we are transformed over time, until the fruits of the Spirit come forth from us like branches on a strong tree.

Fill us with your Spirit and your gifts, Lord, especially in this Lenten season of self-reflection and penitence. May we use those gifts to point the way to you, and to help others see you clearly in the walk to the cross. —LHF

Friday in Lent 2

That it may please thee to bring into the way of truth all such as have erred, and are deceived,

We beseech thee to hear us, good Lord.

Simon Peter saw his limitations more clearly than most people do. Think of that morning scene early in Jesus' ministry on the shore of Lake Gennesaret (Luke 5:1-11). Peter and James and John are on the beach, washing out their nets, having fished all night to no avail. No doubt all they want is to go home and sleep.

But Jesus needs help. People are on his trail, stepping in his path and elbowing close to him, so close that he cannot be heard or seen.

Peter takes him out in the boat so that he can address the people on shore. Finally Jesus remembers that Peter needs fish. Almost as an afterthought he says, "Cast your net over there, in the deep waters."

Peter argues. "We fished all night and caught nothing!" But Jesus encourages him to try. And Peter does. The fish fill the nets and the boats—for Peter has called his friends to help—and they all begin to sink.

"Go forth from me, Lord, for I am a sinful man!" cries Peter.

This is the man that Jesus chooses to lead the church—the one who, after he sees a miracle unfold in front of him, can think of nothing but his own sinfulness.

Perhaps that is an attractive trait in Peter. He had others as well: faithfulness, spontaneity, passion. Jesus thought highly enough of him to eventually name him the rock of the church.

Humility must please God, as does the willingness to go into deep waters. It's a good combination. —*LHF*

Saturday in Lent 2

*That it may please thee to give us a heart to
love and fear thee, and diligently to live after thy
commandments,*

We beseech thee to hear us, good Lord.

Dogs. They know. They get it. They understand
what it means to love and fear at the same time. We
have an Australian shepherd, a big, fluffy, brown
and white, enthusiastic dog. When called, night or
day, he comes running joyfully, wanting to be with
us, trusting that wherever we are going will be a
good place.

That's the love part. Here's the fear part: if
we reprimand him, he backs away, head down, tail
between his legs. He watches us, waiting for the
moment he is forgiven, called back into communion.

His goal is to be in a good relationship with us,
always. He's not happy unless that's the case. He has
committed himself for a lifetime. His pack is our
family.

Human beings are not dogs, of course, and God
doesn't want us to be. Free will, while dogs have it,
is not central to who they are. For human beings,
however, it is central. It seems to be important to God
too, for one of his first acts was to endow creation
with an object of desire and ultimate temptation,

namely the Tree of Knowledge in the Garden of Eden. He didn't have to put it there. Clearly, God endorses choice. He wants us to make up our own minds, to come freely.

Still, we can learn something from our canine companions. A good dog pays attention. He's not about assigning blame. He wants to please. He follows the rules. He comes when he's called. He stays with the pack. He loves unconditionally. He is ready to go anywhere, anytime, following the voice of the one he loves.

Not a bad example to consider during Lent. —*LHF*

Third Sunday in Lent

That it may please thee so to rule the hearts of thy servants, the President of the United States, and all others in authority, that they may do justice, and love mercy, and walk in the ways of truth,

We beseech thee to hear us, good Lord.

The phrase *Gott Mit Uns*, God with Us, was said to have graced the belt buckles of German soldiers in World Wars I and II. *Gott Mit Uns*. God with *us*. But what about God with *them*?

In *The Last Battle*, the final book of C.S. Lewis's Narnia stories, there are two great foes. The one, the Narnians, are said to follow Aslan, the great lion Christ figure. Their opponents, the Telmarines, serve Tash, a heinous bird-like, devouring, destructive lord of war. At the tale's end, not all Narnians get to heaven, and not all Telmarines go down to destruction. Because, it turns out, what matters is who you *really* serve.

Those who followed the good—doing works of compassion and truth, love, kindness, and courage—were really serving Aslan, no matter what name was on their banner. And those who followed evil—selfishness, cowardice, betrayal, destruction—were actually followers of Tash, even if they wore the name of Aslan on their armor.

It matters who rules our hearts, which is what we pray for the President of the United States and for all in authority. We don't pray that God will be on their (and our) side, but that God will rule their (and our) hearts. The direction makes all the difference. In the end we will be known by our fruits.

We pray that we may "do justice, and love mercy, and walk in the ways of truth." That's a good test for our politicians as well as ourselves. —*LWF*

Monday in Lent 3

That it may please thee to make wars to cease in all the world; to give to all nations unity, peace, and concord; and to bestow freedom upon all peoples,

We beseech thee to hear us, good Lord.

Yesterday Presidents, today wars, tomorrow prisoners and the homeless. Cranmer's petitions for this week would seem to focus us upon our common societal life; which is not surprising because Cranmer understood well that our religious and civic lives are intertwined and cannot be disengaged.

A fairly recent (within most of our lifetimes) American tendency has been to view the constitutional separation of church and state as totally disengaging the two realms, but it doesn't work. Human hearts moved by the gospel imperative understand that the benefits of freedom and justice and compassion are meant to be enacted in the larger fabric.

It is demonic when religious motives are co-opted to serve nationalistic ends. But it is also demonic when we dismiss the religious and spiritual aspects of our lives from our common story.

One of the hostages in the 1979 Iranian crisis noted that when they had written to their counterparts in the United States about the religious turmoil and rise of Islamic fundamentalism, they were told to "take that religious stuff out of your reports" and talk only about the "real things"—money, power plays, and who was sleeping with whom...

We Americans got blind-sided because the religious story *was* the real story, and our "radical separation" ignored it to our detriment.

That political rulers will try to use religious impulses toward their own ends is a well-known story, and what the "separation" part is about. But in fact our faith has absolute connections to how we form our societies.

What parts of my faith have I been ignoring in terms of the needs of the world around me? —*LWF*

Tuesday in Lent 3

That it may please thee to show thy pity upon all prisoners and captives, the homeless and the hungry, and all who are desolate and oppressed,

We beseech thee to hear us, good Lord.

At three o'clock in the morning, atop a three-story tier of iron cages in the middle of a concrete shell of a building with only a small flashlight for comfort, I feel scared. "What the heck was I thinking?"

It was 1966 and I was a chaplain intern at San Quentin prison, doing guard duty in the cell blocks as part of orientation. "You're supposed to check and make sure they're in their cells," I was told.

"And what if they're not?" I wondered.

When we pray for prisoners and the homeless, I suspect we often mean the innocent ones, the ones wrongly incarcerated or held by our enemies, or those made homeless and hungry by the bad turns of others. But what if they're not innocent? What if they did the terrible things they were charged with? What if they are homeless and hungry because of their own stupidity and bad choices?

I suspect God would say, "So what?"

We all need forgiveness and pity, even when we are stupid. Maybe particularly when we've been stupid. If we weren't actually in the wrong, we wouldn't need forgiveness. We would have a good excuse.

My time at San Quentin taught me the reality of original sin: that what was in those inmates was in me too, and that we all need to take care. Facing honestly into what we and others might fail at—why we all need help—is an integral part of the Lenten journey.

Thank God that the Lord shows pity upon those who really *are* pitiful. How can I get better at doing that myself? —*LWF*

Wednesday in Lent 3

That it may please thee to give and preserve to our use the bountiful fruits of the earth, so that in due time all may enjoy them,

We beseech thee to hear us, good Lord.

It is a sign of our times that we seem particularly aware of this petition. Global warming, ecological care, green *this* and green *that* are talked about everywhere. The disagreements come when we try to figure out a solution or point the finger of blame.

And one generation's solution can seem like the next's insanity.

It is easy to forget that the automobile and internal combustion engine were seen as saviors of civil health in places like New York City less than a century ago. A hot August day near the Fulton Fish Market in lower Manhattan before refrigeration was a robust aromatic experience, to say the least. And streets filled with gutter stench, as horse droppings and urine flowed down them into the Hudson or East Rivers, were no bundle of healthy laughs either.

Each generation appreciates the bounty of the earth but responds differently. My New England ancestors saw rivers and valleys and saw them improved—the bounty made more fruitful—when they paved them over and built mills on them.

Were they wrong? Are we more right? Politically, even scientifically, I do not know the answer. And maybe only a century-forth generation will know whether our "solutions" really improved things or not.

What I do know is that I am very appreciative of the bountiful fruits of the earth. They are a gift to us from the Lord of life, and we need to work so that all indeed may enjoy them, rather than just a lucky few. —*LWF*

Thou openest thy hand O Lord in due season....

—Psalm 104:28-29

Thursday in Lent 3

That it may please thee to inspire us, in our several callings, to do the work which thou givest us to do with singleness of heart as thy servants, and for the common good,

We beseech thee to hear us, good Lord.

In our "several callings." When I first approached retirement I had a limited sense of call. I realize that now. After forty years in the ordained ministry I saw that as my call, and I was anxious about leaving my call behind.

Looking back, it is clear how misled I was! I have had several callings all along the way of my life. If anything, retirement has given me the opportunity to delve more intentionally and fully into some of the others that my "official" ministry had pushed to the side over the years.

All along, I have been called—to be a father to my children, a support to my spouse, a writer, a doer of laundry and shopping, a consultant and guide for others in their ministries, a friend, and an analyzer of movies, books, and the arts, looking for the touch of God's hand in them. The list goes on.

The point of it is that *at all times and in all places,* you and I have signed up to be parts of the Body of Christ. When I do the family shopping I am just as called and just as able to exercise my faith with my choices as when I write a sermon or say a prayer with a friend in the hospital.

I find it freeing to realize my different callings. It lets me enter into the different parts of my particular life story and know their value. This allows me to offer my whole self up, "with a singleness of heart."

—*LWF*

Friday in Lent 3

That it may please thee to preserve all who are in danger by reason of their labor or their travel,

We beseech thee to hear us, good Lord.

I grew up in a New England mill town, where some of my friends paid the price. Because labor has its dangers. One of my best friends, Bobby, never made it out of town. After marrying his high school sweetheart he went to work in those mills, where early on a machine ripped off his right hand. He couldn't work there any longer, and things spiraled downhill. Early in his forties Bobby was found by the side of a park we used to play in together as kids, dead from a heroin overdose.

None of us were little angels. A sneaked snitch of alcohol was the drug of choice when we were kids. So maybe Bobby would have had his troubles anyway, but it always struck me that the dangers of his labor were what tipped the whole thing over.

Work is hard. Work can be dangerous. And whether physically or emotionally, we need to look out for each other there. Because it's not just about making the money. It's about our souls.

When it goes right, work can be enormously fulfilling and joyful; genuinely a gift to us of calling.

But even then, we need to honor and appreciate the prices people may pay in getting the job done.

One of the dangers of labor in our current economy may well be the lack of it, for what it does to a man or woman in our society when their work is taken away. "Downsized" is such a bland euphemism. It still means that you are out of work. And to not be able to labor is its own danger.

How can we help one another, support one another, through these dangerous times? It's not about the money. It's about our souls. —*LWF*

Saturday in Lent 3

That it may please thee to preserve, and provide for, all women in childbirth, young children and orphans, the widowed, and all whose homes are broken or torn by strife,

We beseech thee to hear us, good Lord.

Halfway through Lent is a good time to stop for a status check. When Ed Koch was mayor of New York City he would walk up to people on the street and ask: "How'm I doing?"

You and I probably don't need to take to the streets. On the other hand, as citizens of the kingdom, and working on it, what would those in need around us say if we asked them, "How'm I doing?" Would they see us as progressing? Or is it still the same old, same old?

Not a bad gut check, as they say.

The daily media provide us with images of the most vulnerable, those whom Cranmer calls to our attention today. In his time, when men were the primary bread winners and the family was as much an economic institution as a social one, homes broken by the absence or death of a male were in serious jeopardy.

We have become more egalitarian in terms of equal work for equal pay, but has life really gotten that much better for those who are vulnerable?

The poor and the vulnerable will always be with us. Jesus said that. I don't think he meant that we should throw up our hands and walk away, but that we will never lack the opportunity to be God's hands and hearts for those in need.

I know that I am on my own soul's journey, as I reflect upon it this Lent. But as Jesus makes clear, my journey is linked to theirs.

How'm I doing? —*LWF*

Fourth Sunday in Lent

That it may please thee to visit the lonely; to strengthen all who suffer in mind, body, and spirit; and to comfort with thy presence those who are failing and infirm,

We beseech thee to hear us, good Lord.

Among the houses on Lake Minnetonka was a dark shack. Dark inside and out, as I was soon to see. A woman named Gladys lived there, so crippled from arthritis that she could barely move, crippled and unable to see much. Perhaps she was totally blind; I don't know. I was about eight years old.

The house smelled bad. Gladys smelled bad. Somehow my mother felt called to visit her weekly, to bring her food, even to empty the coffee can that Gladys used as an occasional toilet. All I wanted to do was to play outside, away from the darkness, in the sun and lake-wafted air.

And then we'd go to see the next person on the list, a woman in an iron lung. She lay encased in a steel tube and could only see us by looking at a mirror positioned over her head. Sometimes we'd visit a mother whose twelve-year-old son had leukemia and who had his own stairlift built into the side of his hill so that he could ride to the lake below.

Compassion was apparently not one of my strong suits as a child, for life and death and arthritis and leukemia were not easy things to assimilate. But such visits now bring me great joy and are part of my vocation as an adult. I strive to bring comfort; I almost always leave feeling closer to God. Perhaps I was paying more attention than I thought.

May we all find ways to teach the youngest among us this Lent, knowing that the really important things are often taught outside the classroom. —*LHF*

Monday in Lent 4

That it may please thee to support, help, and comfort all who are in danger, necessity, and tribulation,

We beseech thee to hear us, good Lord.

I had a blessedly adventurous teacher in high school. An Outward Bound instructor, he took about thirty of us, once a year, on trips around the United States in old school buses.

One of our projects was to hike part of the Appalachian Trail in the Great Smoky Mountains National Park. Off to a late start because we had to wait for a park ranger's inspection, we started the long trek up into the mountains shortly before noon.

And there, ten miles up, the sky broke open, drenching us in a mixture of cold rain and snow. Darkness fell and we had yet to reach the huts that would provide shelter. We were without tents. Wet, cold, and scared, we kept going.

I wound up at the back of the line of the last group, at the mercy of the slow-footed overweight hiker in front of me, having been encouraged to make sure no one got lost in the black night.

Voices from up the line became dim. And that is when I learned that strength doesn't always mean you are out in front. Sometimes you use it when no one sees it, when your job is to follow others, helping them to have confidence in their own strides. Sometimes you can do more good at the end of the line than in the front, as humility takes over ego.

We're never really alone in the back; Someone else walks beside us. But as God provides us with help and support, he also gives us new lessons to learn. —*LHF*

Tuesday in Lent 4

That it may please thee to have mercy upon all mankind,

We beseech thee to hear us, good Lord.

Surely such a plea can't mean mercy for the absolute worst of the human race. Surely not criminals, like the man in the news today who was arrested for repeatedly raping children. Surely not the man who abducted a young woman from her job as a convenience store cashier, drove her away, and killed her. Surely not Osama Bin Laden and other terrorists who seek to destroy this country and those we love.

Hmmm…mercy upon all mankind. *All* mankind. And not a grudging mercy. We want God to be "pleased" to show mercy to all mankind.

When I'm angry with someone, when it's all I can do to pray—and even that is hard if I'm really angry—the prayer often takes the form of throwing that person into a room like a cave, semi-dark, with no exit. I drag him or her in there mentally, or find a ledge and push the offender into the space below.

And then I walk away. Only I haven't left the person alone; Jesus is there, too. And Jesus works it out.

So we pray. We pray for God truly to have mercy on all mankind, the worst and best of the lot. Moreover, we pray that God will be "pleased" to have mercy.

Jesus is in the room, so we can walk away at least having done what God has asked, and that is to pray for our enemies and those who offend us.

God, have mercy on us all. Fill us with your Spirit, and when we have run out of our own limited compassion and kindness, mercifully grant us those gifts through your Son.—LHF

Wednesday in Lent 4

That it may please thee to give us true repentance; to forgive us all our sins, negligences, and ignorances; and to endue us with the grace of thy Holy Spirit to amend our lives according to thy holy Word,

We beseech thee to hear us, good Lord.

Jonah is one of my favorite biblical characters. He runs away from God because God wants him to convince the people of Ninevah to repent. He hates the Ninevites, and with good reason. They kill; they maim; they ruin the lives of everyone they touch. God intends that, through Jonah's preaching, they will be converted.

But Jonah does not want the Ninevites to repent. He wants them destroyed. If they repent, God will give them another chance.

As we know, Jonah hops onto a fishing boat that is conveniently sailing the other way. But the sea—i.e., God—doesn't give up. Soon Jonah is pitched into the water and swallowed by a fish who happens to be cruising by. After three days of begging for God's mercy, Jonah is delivered.

Jonah is no lamebrain. He goes to Ninevah and preaches. That should be the end of it. It's not. He gets angry with God because the Ninevites *do* repent.

Jonah is a whiner, a difficult personality. But it doesn't matter to God. God puts him to work and never abandons him.

Difficult people show up throughout biblical history. Simon Peter was incredibly impatient. King David committed adultery with Bathsheba and then arranged for her husband to die in battle. Rebecca lied so that Jacob might receive his father's blessing.

It's about love, God's love. It has to be. Otherwise we would all be lost to the belly of the fish, never to see the light of day. —*LHF*

Thursday in Lent 4

That it may please thee to forgive our enemies,
persecutors, and slanderers, and to turn their hearts,

We beseech thee to hear us, good Lord.

Corrie ten Boom, the well-known Dutch Christian, once wrote, "Forgiveness is to set a prisoner free, and to realize that prisoner was you."

She would know, having been beaten and imprisoned in concentration camps for hiding Jews and helping them escape the Holocaust. Such work was not taken up lightly. It was inspired by her father, who, because of his faithful Bible study, believed that Jews were God's chosen people and thus deserved freedom and protection. So the Ten Boom family altered their house specifically to shield Jewish refugees, adding a secret chamber behind Corrie's bedroom.

Eventually they were betrayed. Corrie's father and sister died at the hands of the Nazis. Corrie herself was severely beaten, but she remembered her sister's final words: "There is no pit so deep that God's love is not deeper still."

Released on a clerical error—the other women her age were killed the following week—she tells of how, at a church following the war, she encountered a concentration camp guard who had tormented her.

He walked up, inspired by her witness, and put out his hand to shake hers in a gesture of newfound faith. Momentarily immobilized, she prayed. In that moment she found transformation and was able to forgive.

"It is not on our forgiveness any more than on our goodness that the world's healing hinges, but on His. When He tells us to love our enemies, He gives, along with the command, the love itself," writes Corrie ten Boom.

May it always be so. —*LHF*

Friday in Lent 4

That it may please thee to strengthen such as do stand; to comfort and help the weak-hearted; to raise up those who fall; and finally to beat down Satan under our feet,

We beseech thee to hear us, good Lord.

Strengthen those who stand. Comfort and help the weak. Raise up the fallen. Beat down Satan. Is there a better mission statement than this for the church? Not likely.

Although God is named above as the primary agent *doing* the work, Teresa of Avila had it right when she said:

Christ has no body now but yours,
No hands, no feet on earth but yours.
Yours are the eyes through which He looks
    compassion on this world.
Christ has no body now on earth but yours.

And the part about Satan? That's what makes it more than the purpose statement of any good-hearted secular agency. In a day when Satan's name is rarely mentioned, perhaps Martin Luther said things best in his famous hymn "A Mighty Fortress Is Our God":

And though this world, with devils filled,
    should threaten to undo us;
we will not fear, for God hath willed
    his truth to triumph through us;
the prince of darkness grim, we tremble not for him;
his rage we can endure, for lo! his doom is sure,
    one little word shall fell him.

That word above all earthly powers,
    no thanks to them, abideth;
the Spirit and the gifts are ours
    through him who with us sideth:
let goods and kindred go, this mortal life also;
the body they may kill: God's truth abideth still,
    his kingdom is for ever.

—THE HYMNAL 1982, #687
—LHF

Saturday in Lent 4

That it may please thee to grant to all the faithful departed eternal life and peace,

We beseech thee to hear us, good Lord.

Our Christian faith is different. Different from those faith traditions that say all that matters is this life, the here and now.

Several years ago, our congregation finished a columbarium, which provides for the interment of cremated remains next to the church. There is room for the ashes of three thousand people, but only one wall listing the names, and there was only room for one sentence to be engraved on the wall.

How does one find a sentence to both summarize our faith and to comfort those visiting the graves of loved ones? We chose this phrase from Romans 8: "Nothing can separate us from the love of God in Christ Jesus."

Paul writes about it in more detail: "For I am convinced that neither death, nor life, nor angels, nor rulers, nor things present, nor things to come, nor powers, nor height, nor depth, nor anything else in all creation, will be able to separate us from the love of God in Christ Jesus our Lord" (Romans 8:38-39).

Nothing can separate us from the love of God. Nothing, especially death. Jesus holds us close and he holds close all those who have died in the faith, including our loved ones. We *will* see them again.

We know more. In John 14, Jesus tells Thomas and the rest of the disciples that he is going to prepare a place for them, a house with many rooms, and that he will return to take them with him.

Nothing can separate us. Jesus has prepared a place for us. We will see the ones we love. The shepherd will accompany us.

In this Lenten season, as we approach the cross, it is good news. Very good news, indeed. *—LHF*

Fifth Sunday in Lent

That it may please thee to grant that, in the fellowship of all the saints, we may attain to thy heavenly kingdom,

We beseech thee to hear us, good Lord.

It comes around in the end that we too hope to spend eternity with the good guys, in the fellowship of the saints. Through these thirty-two petitions Thomas Cranmer has taken us through a virtual soul's tour of human concern and longings. Most notable is how current and present are the voices that reach out to us from this oldest portion of *The Book of Common Prayer*.

For all our shifts in knowledge—science, technology, and the social sciences—the elements remain pretty much the same in terms of the growth of our souls. Which is why you and I can go back to ancient documents such as these and hear in them the Word of God.

Shaking hands at the back of one church or another after a service over the years, I have often had the experience of someone saying about my sermon: "I really liked when you said such-and-so." I would smile, nod and think: "I don't recall saying such-and-so. *That* wasn't my point!"

I used to worry that I hadn't expressed myself clearly enough, until it struck me one day that *my* point wasn't the point. God uses everything—the ancient words of the Bible, the words out of my mouth, the stained glass, prayer books and hymn texts, as well as the thoughts going through people's heads specific to their particular lives—to speak to the longings and concerns of our hearts. Things can change in their external specifics, but they remain the same in their internal, and eternal, goal: "I want to be in that number, when the saints go marching in." —*LWF*

Monday in Lent 5

The Story of Creation —GENESIS 1:1—2:2

O God, who wonderfully created, and more wonderfully restored, the dignity of human nature...
—*THE BOOK OF COMMON PRAYER, P. 288*

"Tell me a story, Daddy. Tell me a story!" I was very little, wide-eyed, and happy. Because my dad, whose day job was as a machinist in the mills, was at home. The most wonderful story-teller, he would spin me tales at bedtime straight out of his head. Of Mr. Tinsnips who, with just a few fast snip-snaps of his shears, would craft a wonderful toy or implement that would make the little boy in the story happy and save the day. Of Mrs. Putty Pants and many others.

Perhaps it's why I still go to stories as my primary avenue for engaging life. Early on I knew that my daddy was letting me in on something special with his creativity, a touch of something divine. And it was my best of all best times with him.

The stories get different as we get older, but they are still evidence of the creative spark at the heart of our own story. This is why, when we need to touch down to realities that speak to us, we go back to them. In a novel, or a film, or a television series—or the Bible.

Beginning today, our reflections look ahead to Easter Eve. "Let us hear the record of God's saving deeds in history," we say as the Easter Vigil begins its narration of lessons. The Creation story follows. And starting with Creation is right—not just because it takes us to "In the beginning," but because it connects us to the creative touch that moves in each of us, and to which our hearts respond, as a primal connector to the divine.

What creativity livens your path these days? What creation do you express? —*LWF*

Tuesday in Lent 5

The Flood —Genesis 7:1-5, 11-18; 8:6-18; 9:8-13

Almighty God, you have placed in the skies the sign of your covenant with all living things...
                              —*The Book of Common Prayer*, p. 289

The animals came in two by two. The versions of the Flood story I have heard since childhood usually have disbelieving people mocking Noah as he goes about building the ark, "three hundred cubits by fifty cubits by thirty cubits high." Noah ignores the disdain and goes ahead with his project because even if only he hears it, the voice of the Lord tells him truth.

It is a wonderful image—the true-believing Noah ignoring the catcalls from the neighbors and, of course, the unbelievers literally drowning in their mistakenness once they realize that Noah is right. Perfect moral teaching for us good Protestant kids raised, even if we didn't know it, in the spirit of Martin Luther: "Here I stand, I can do no other." The lone individual, standing up against the mob, is a mythos deep within our individualistic American heritage.

The only problem is that none of that interchange appears in the Bible. No neighbors, no disdain or catcalls, no heroic standing against the crowd.

So what *is* the point? A warning about ecological disaster? A vague remembrance of a Mediterranean cataclysm of human prehistory and how we survived it?

This is a story about the fact that we are all in this together. It is a covenant with *all* creation. And the simple but clear point is that, even if all the world seems corrupted, God's purposes will not be defeated. It is a story of hopefulness and promise for all creation, based on God's assurance that, in the end, destruction will not *be* the end.

Keeps me going. —*LWF*

Wednesday in Lent 5

Abraham's sacrifice of Isaac —GENESIS 22:1-18

God and Father of all believers...

—THE BOOK OF COMMON PRAYER, P. 289

I was in an ancient Irish churchyard looking over a stone wall that had been blackened and swept soft by the wind and rain of centuries. Sheltered within stood Christian and Druidic gravestones side by side. Ancient Celtic crossed markers intermingled with hole-pierced obelisks, a silent testament to the passing of one tradition to another.

Standing there, I had a sense that our Christian faith was able to convert the Druidic peoples because we spoke their language. We understood sacrifice, but came with a new message: the sacrifice had been taken care of, once and for all; we no longer have to kill our children.

The Genesis story is really the story of Abraham's *non*-sacrifice of Isaac. Thank God he doesn't actually do the boy in. Thank God, because God does not ask this of us, even if we sometimes think he does, even if we sometimes "hear" voices that seem to demand such things.

Some scholars cite the parallelism between the father/son story of Abraham and Isaac and the Father/Son story of Calvary. Jerusalem, some believe, is built atop the same mountain that Abraham ascended to sacrifice Isaac. But that thought does not bring me comfort. Because the message for you and me is that God does not ask this of us. Whatever is going on, *that* has been dealt with.

In an age that can "eat its young"—for what else is it if we so mortgage our children's future that they will have lesser lives beacuse of our profligacy—it is an important truth. The real Lord neither asks nor approves of such behaviors. Only the false gods of mammon and greed, of acquisition and thoughtlessness do. —*LWF*

Thursday in Lent 5

Israel's deliverance at the Red Sea
—Exodus 14:10—15:1

O God, whose wonderful deeds of old shine forth...
—*The Book of Common Prayer*, p. 289

Deliverance.

After we have gained some awareness of our origins—our Genesis stories—the next step in the spiritual life is to gain a sense of our deliverance, our Exodus out of some disaster where we had been lain waste, to a new place.

Our initial sense of "other"—God, creator, mother, father, ground of being, whatever—can fade. Was it just wishful thinking? A projection? A warm story like Santa and the Easter Bunny that we are meant to grow out of?

Then disaster strikes and we are oppressed and brought low. Maybe we are not slaves in Egypt, but we're slaves to something. A job disaster, a natural disaster, a health issue, the end of a relationship...

Every life has its own story. But somewhere along the way, standing at the edge of a Red Sea of our own or another's devising, it becomes clear that we need deliverance. When deliverance comes, it becomes to the eyes of faith one of the "wonderful deeds of old"—the living experience of a change—that shapes the rest of our days.

In John Updike's book *Couples*, there is a man who has lost his job. Others see him as someone to be pitied. But the narrator, watching the man puttering in his garden one morning, realizes that he doesn't come across as broken. Rather he appears as someone who has fallen to the depths and found the bottom to be solid and whole.

Deliverance comes in many ways. The core miracle is our experience of God's active hand getting us through the waters to dry land—even if we've had to wander years in the desert, on our way to the promised land. —*LWF*

Friday in Lent 5

God's Presence in a renewed Israel —ISAIAH 4:2-6

O God...we, who serve you now on earth...
                                    —*THE BOOK OF COMMON PRAYER*, P. 290

Forty years ago I sat in the unfinished nave of Washington National Cathedral and listened to Dr. Martin Luther King Jr. deliver what would be his last sermon. I was there to hear about the civil rights struggle. So when Dr. King started to talk about our national involvement in Vietnam, I thought: "Where is this coming from? What does this have to do with anything? This is crazy!"

My impression, of course, was wrong. He was being a prophet, a voice expressing God's presence and vision for the renewal of our culture.

God's presence in ancient Israel, creating and renewing the nation, was initially experienced through the Ten Commandments. Much like our Constitution, the Commandments took those who were "no people" and formed them into God's people, with a land, a vision, and a rule of law. For hundreds of years there would be no kings for Israel, because God was the King.

At the dissolution of that nation, the diaspora, a new vehicle of divine presence emerged, the prophets:

Isaiah, Joel, Ezekiel, and others. They spoke of hope, they spoke of warning, and they presented a look at the world through God's eyes, extending his promise into the context of their uprooted places and times.

It still works that way. God comes among us through prophetic voices for the same purpose: the renewal of nations and peoples and cultures gone astray or in despair.

I don't always "get" these voices at first. Sometimes they sound crazy. But my prayer is that, over the years, I have learned to look and listen with a little more openness for the presence of the Lord. *—LWF*

Saturday in Lent 5

Salvation offered freely to all —ISAIAH 55:1-11

O God...Give now the water of life to those who thirst for you...

—THE BOOK OF COMMON PRAYER, P. 290

Family fights can be the worst.

That God opens his loving arms for everyone can seem obvious. It is fashionable nowadays to appear tolerant toward other religions—Buddhism, Islam, Judaism, even nonbelievers and pagans. But when it's within the family, other Christians who oppose what I view as "correct" or practice their religion in ways that I see as "oppressive," it can seem as if all bets are off.

Some of the nastiest fighting and mean-spirited shunning I have experienced have come from within the church—within a congregation where one parishioner will not sit on a committee if another is present because of some previous disagreement or slight, or among clergy who have different agendas.

Coming up on Holy Week, where people of God will turn on the Son of God, Isaiah's words of salvation offered freely to all speak volumes. God offers salvation even to those who see the world differently than I do. And he even seems to love them. Amazing.

That is the point. "Love so amazing, so divine," as the old hymn puts it, is actually a lot more than I am used to, or perhaps capable of. Which is why I need God's help at getting this right. And it is why Holy Week will lead us not to a program or a philosophy, but to God's intervention in our behalf to make a difference.

At some level we all thirst, we all hunger, and none of us has it right. "Come to me, all you that are weary and are carrying heavy burdens, and I will give you rest," says Jesus (Matthew 11:28). He really does say *all*. —LWF

Palm Sunday

Blessed is the one who comes in the name of the Lord!
—Matthew 21:9

It is no wonder that ashes are made from palms. Once lively, green, and bendable, palms are put away after Palm Sunday and then burnt months later for Ash Wednesday, becoming a sign of brokenness and humility.

From green to gray. From life to death.

Such a transformation is symbolic of what Jesus faces during Holy Week. The residents of Jerusalem cheer his coming, raise palms to honor him, and throw down their cloaks to protect him from the dust and dirt of the road. Days later, he is dead.

His first act after being hailed by the crowds is to throw out the merchants and their customers doing business in the temple. Then in Matthew's Gospel there is a small, often overlooked line: "Then he returned to Bethany, where he stayed overnight."

Two miles outside of Jerusalem, in the sleepy town of Bethany, Jesus had friends: Mary and Martha and Lazarus. Somehow in the grief and craziness of the week, Jesus found solace and comfort with them.

In Bethany, Martha made wonderful meals and provided lodging for Jesus and his friends. It was there, much to her sister's chagrin, that Mary sat unmoving at Jesus' feet, listening with her whole heart. It was there that Jesus raised Lazarus from the dead, and Mary poured the perfumed oil over Jesus' feet.

One more thing about the sleepy town and the small band of friends: Jesus came back there to ascend to heaven.

Clearly Jesus doesn't forget his friends, the ones who have given him particular comfort, solace, and strength. By what we do and by who we are, may we also be counted in that sacred circle. —LHF

Monday in Holy Week

A new heart and a new spirit —Ezekiel 26:24-28

Almighty and everlasting God...Grant that all who are reborn into the fellowship of Christ's Body may show forth in their lives what they profess by their faith. —THE BOOK OF COMMON PRAYER, p. 290

Some people are in love with oceans. Not me. Lake Superior, along Minnesota's north shore, has my heart instead. I've been going back to it since high school. One summer in college, a friend and I lived in a cabin there that had neither electricity nor running water.

We didn't need either. We had candles and lanterns and one-tenth of the world's fresh water just yards from the back door. We drew water to drink; we put perishables in a lakeside bucket, tied it shut, and weighed it down with a rock. Sometimes it worked; other times we lost a piece of cheese or a container of orange juice to the deep.

Each night as I went to sleep I could hear the waves lap against two-billion-year-old bedrock. In, out. In, out.

Over the years, I have come to think of that sound as the breath of God, a holy sound indeed. As God separated the firmament from the chaos at Creation, before he breathed life into dust and made human beings, perhaps his own breath was heard on earth for the first time, as the first waves found their mark.

In today's reading from Ezekiel, God tells his people that he will pour water all over them and scrub them clean. Being drowned to sin and scrubbed clean is a good analogy for Holy Week.

Where's the holy water in your life? Where do you hear the breath of God? Try to find it as part of your walk to the cross this week. —*LHF*

Tuesday in Holy Week

The valley of dry bones —Ezekiel 37:1-14

Almighty God...you have brought us...out of death into life. —*The Book of Common Prayer, p. 291*

Many years ago, I worked for St. Martin's-in-the-Fields, Chestnut Hill, Philadelphia, a congregation with a strong tradition of celebrating the Easter Vigil.

When the story of the valley of the dry bones came up, Margaret, a tiny white-haired woman, would read it. When she got to the part about the bones coming together, she would take a deep breath and proclaim, "There was a *ratt*-ling!"

Heads would pop up. We would smile. Somewhere deep in her soul, what she knew about pain and loss and God all came together. Through her faith, she helped us imagine dry bones being raised up and knit together, limb to limb, sinew to sinew. An army of God's elect would be raised and would march forth, full of spirit and life, dusty and lifeless no longer. We could almost see them, their bones rattling as they stood up, full of hope and breath and health.

And so could the Babylonian captives from Israel to whom Ezekiel first preached these words, giving them hope. Hope that God still loved them after the destruction of the temple in Jerusalem. Hope that one day they might return refreshed and whole to their home, no longer strangers in a strange land. Hope that all tears would be wiped from their eyes and their children would again grow strong and free, full of hope and faith.

Resurrection. We take it for granted now. But what would it be like to lose loved ones and be without hope of ever seeing them again? Thanks to Jesus, they will stand again, and we will be among them, full of life and breath. —*LHF*

Wednesday in Holy Week

The gathering of God's people —ZEPHANIAH 3:12-20

O God...Look favorably on your whole Church, that wonderful and sacred mystery...
—*THE BOOK OF COMMON PRAYER*, P. 291

The church, that "wonderful and sacred mystery." The church, that confusing and obdurate rabble. The church, you and me, all these years later still trying to get it right.

The church is indeed a mystery, of God's continuing love and patience and promise toward us. There are days when I throw my hands up at the failings of the institution, and others when I emerge from a worship service lifted up, renewed, and changed for the day.

This final Vigil lesson from Zephaniah, written six hundred years before Christ, provides a simple promise. The Lord will gather "a people humble and lowly," who "shall do no wrong and utter no lies, nor shall a deceitful tongue be found in their mouths... they will pasture and lie down, and no one shall make them afraid" (Zephaniah 3:12-13).

What a vision! If only we could be like that. Simple. Clear. Honest. Caring. Unaffected. And unafraid.

I think I would like to spend an eternity with people like this. I pray that the Lord will help me get better at being like this. And with God's grace, I believe I can.

Jesuit scholar Walter Ong talks about the masks, the positive images of ourselves that we present to the world, as being not false fronts but things that draw us to them. Pretend to be a better person than you are, and in time the mask will draw you toward becoming that reality.

You and I could do much worse than to wear the mask of that "wonderful and sacred mystery," of "a people humble and lowly" who "do no wrong and utter no lies." —*LWF*

Maundy Thursday

The Lord Jesus, after he had supped with his disciples and had washed their feet, said to them, "Do you know what I, your Lord and Master, have done to you? I have given you an example, that you should do as I have done."

—*THE BOOK OF COMMON PRAYER*, P. 274

When I was first ordained I learned a piece of Anglican theology that has stuck with me. As a priest, I have been authorized to consecrate the bread and wine of the eucharist as the body and blood of Christ on behalf of the church. But it only "works" if there are others present. A priest saying the words of institution alone does not "produce" the body and blood of Christ. Others must be gathered.

The two mandates (maundy) of this day then— "Do this in remembrance of me" (1 Corinthians 11:24) and "I have set you an example, that you also should do as I have done to you" (John 13:15)—involve other people.

You can't do eucharist by yourself, even if you are ordained. And we can't imitate Christ without some others to serve.

Our Lenten journey—the Christian journey— turns out to be not an individualized, personal quest, but a movement out of our selves into relation with others. We share a group faith. It's really that simple. And both of Christ's final commandments take us to each other.

Jesus is saying to us: Eat this bread, drink this cup, together, and I will be there with you. Do whatever is needful to care for each other—for nothing is too lowly for us to do in the care of one another—and you will be doing as I have done for you.

So how are we doing with that? We asked ourselves that question somewhere about mid-Lent. It's worth asking again. —*LWF*

Good Friday

Our Lord Jesus Christ was willing to be betrayed, and given into the hands of sinners, and to suffer death upon the cross...

—*THE BOOK OF COMMON PRAYER, P. 276*

Christ died for our sins. That is why this day of crucifixion is called "Good" in our tradition. Because Christ died for *our* sins.

How seriously do I take that?

This morning's newspaper had a front page story about five teenagers in Newark, New Jersey, who disappeared twenty-eight years ago. They drove off in the back of the pickup truck of a local handyman and were never heard from again.

The case was solved this week. The handyman came forward and confessed that he and two friends had kidnapped the five for stealing some marijuana, tied them up in a deserted building, and burned it to the ground. The ensuing inferno destroyed all traces of the boys and the crime.

Deep in the story a single line explained how the case was solved and the parents' questions finally answered. The handyman confessed because he said that "he'd become a born-again Christian, and so he had to tell the truth."

I think of the thief on the cross with Jesus, the one whom Jesus told "today you will be with me in Paradise." There is a tendency to see him as a basically good person. But what if he wasn't? What if he and this handyman were essentially the same person?

It gives me pause. Because many of us confuse forgiveness with excusing. But if there is an excuse, if we say, "I only did it because of XYZ," then forgiveness is not really what we're asking for or what we are going to get.

It is when we walk away from our excuses and face into our real culpability for what we've done wrong that the Lord has something to say to us.

And when we're at our worst? I give thanks that Christ died for my sins. —*LWF*

Holy Saturday

This is the night, when you brought our fathers, the children of Israel, out of bondage in Egypt...

This is the night, when all who believe in Christ, are delivered from the gloom of sin, and are restored to grace and holiness of life.

This is the night, when Christ broke the bonds of death and hell, and rose victorious from the grave.

—*THE BOOK OF COMMON PRAYER*, P. 287

There is a popular Christian greeting for the morning that comes from Psalm 118: "This is the day that the Lord has made; let us rejoice and be glad in it." It expresses our appreciation for creation and our anticipation of the potential in every day.

But what about the night, the dark times through which our souls pass, the difficulties, struggles, and heartache? These too are times of the Lord. Coming through them is perhaps even more indicative of the reality of Christian life, the experience of a night in which dark, evil, hurtful things are overcome. And the deliverance changes us.

Israel looked back to its deliverance from Pharoah's pursuing armies at the Red Sea. We look back to Christ's deliverance from death upon the cross, and its resonance in times of deliverance in our own lives, from "the gloom of sin" and our restoration to "grace and holiness of life."

The nights of my life are but pale echoes of *the* night which is Christ's night. But they connect my soul with its living truth. The birth of a first child after a hard night of labor that turned into emergency surgery. The emergence of a new relationship after the failure of a marriage. The restoration of health after months of desperate pain from the breaking down of a body.

Our experiences of deliverance send us forth changed, different. And that is what the word "holy" means: set apart, different from the way we used to be. The same. Yet different. Born anew.

This is *the* night. But we each have our own. What are yours? —*LWF*

Forty Days of Lent

Easter Day

Mary Magdalene went and announced to the disciples, "I have seen the Lord."

—JOHN 20:18

Before the sun rises, Mary Magdalene and the other women begin a cold, dark, dangerous walk to the tomb, carrying spices to anoint Jesus so that his body may be preserved, cared for, treasured.

Dreams shattered, his body is all they have left.

And now even that is gone. The tomb, that place where they were to work quietly and shed more tears, is empty. They are left without his remains. And worse, they are left without hope.

Mary stands alone, doubled over, in grief her anger rising. Had this man just been one more thief in her life, stealing her soul along with her beliefs?

She hears a voice.

"Mary."

Don't bother me now, gardener! Leave me alone! What else can go wrong?

"Mary."

She whirls around, ready to scream. And then she sees him there, smiling.

In that moment, she understands—as much as one can understand heaven and earth and angelic witnesses and cosmic unfoldings. She runs to him, arms open.

"Don't cling to me, Mary. Don't cling. Go and find my brothers. Tell them I am ascending to my Father."

It is hard, but it is enough. He has neither abandoned her nor lied to her. He has come back, alive, all tears wiped from his face, divine Light in front of her.

What was lost has been found. What was thought to have been a betrayal has become a shining light of hope. What was dead is now raised from the dead. Forever, full of joy.

Alleluia. The Lord is risen. The Lord is risen, indeed. Alleluia. —*LHF*

Leonard Freeman and Lindsay Hardin Freeman are Episcopal priests, a married couple and, between them, have won over fifty awards for excellence in religious journalism. They are currently serving as interim rectors at Trinity Church in Excelsior, Minnesota. Len retired as rector of St. Martin's Episcopal Church in Minnetonka Beach, Minnesota, after forty years in parish, print, and television ministries. Lindsay, whose most recent book is *The Scarlet Cord: Conversations with God's Chosen Women* (O Books, London, 2010) has served parishes in Massachusetts, Pennsylvania, and Minnesota, and is the former editor of *Vestry Papers*.